Borrowed Breath

VERA OGDEN BAKKER

authorHOUSE®

AuthorHouse™
1663 Liberty Drive
Bloomington, IN 47403
www.authorhouse.com
Phone: 1-800-839-8640

Published by AuthorHouse   11/22/2014

ISBN: 978-1-4969-5494-7 (sc)
ISBN: 978-1-4969-5493-0 (e)

Library of Congress Control Number: 2014921169

Contents

OUR HOME

COMPANIONS

LIQUID ASSETS

ROTATION

Borrowed Breath

And the Lord God formed man...
and breathed into his nostrils
the breath of life... Genesis 2:7

We all live on borrowed breath,
an allotment given to each man –
some more, some less.

According to God's plan,
fish swim the sea,
animals roam the land,
birds fill the sky,
plants grow everywhere,
and man is given dominion.

Willing or not
we share this earth with all life,
until our last breath
returns to its Source,
where we must account
for our stewardship.

Our Home

In Her Hands

They live on a spacious estate
with no work or worries,
every desire at their fingertips.
Luscious fruits appease their hunger.

As they stroll hand in hand,
he picks a hibiscus blossom,
tucks it in her hair.
She weaves him a garland
of honeysuckle.

They memorize the song of larks,
tickle the cats,
rest on moss covered stones,
drink from cool streams.
At night, they dance with the moon,
call the stars by name.
Rain rustles the leaves
and they laugh.
Fear is unknown.

One day, she catches a glimpse
of eternity
and takes a bite that
changes the world forever.

Earth Song

Your ears will never hear
the earth singing,
for it plays on the same frequency
as a black hole.

Wind whistles wispy clouds
over purple mountains
with the song,
and whispers it
beneath quiet mushrooms.
Rain and snow polka
or waltz to the beat,
as they fall.

Ocean waves dance in tune
and arctic ice flows with lyrics.
Starfish attached to the rocks
listen with unseeing eyes.

Moss draped trees sway
with the rhythm.
Cacti absorb and store
the score for days of drought.

Eagles know the music.
They hold their wings to listen,
while bluebirds and larks
join in ecstatic choruses.
Loons on the lake and owls at night
echo melancholy melodies.

Bats tune their radar
to its wave length,
and snakes slither
to the pulse in their bellies.
A fawn in the forest
naps to its crooning lullaby.

Your ears will never
hear the song,
but if your fingers
probe deep enough
and long enough
into earth's loamy pulse,
they may hear it.

Natural Therapy

The tension of the day is unbearable:
my need to escape, undeniable.

The first leg of my journey
takes me through a field of ragweed.
My eyes run and I sneeze
before I reach the forest,
where air is pine fresh.
A bluebird sings welcome
and ferns wave as I pass.
A field of lupine and daisies
soothe my troubled eyes.
The gurgle of water beckons me on.
Around noon I stop to rest
and eat my lunch near the brook,
I hike upstream past a small waterfall.
In a quiet clearing I make camp.
Soon hotdogs sizzle over my campfire,
and s'mores drizzle down my chin.

Sitting by the crackling fire,
I watch the moon climb
through the fringe of forest.
Stars poke holes in heaven's cover.
An owl hoots. I hear
soft scurrying sounds in the forest.

I am such a small part
in the scheme of things
and there is no sign of tension.

Voices of the Night

The summer moon begins its evening climb
above the purple mountain, paints its glow
on blackened face of night. Dark crickets prime
their churrs. The hoots of waking owls now flow
on wings of swoop and grab survival. Cats
bemoan their aching plight in whining air.
Against my window fleeting shapes of bats
appear. Across my pillow, bugs of care
and nightly terrors creep. Unfounded fear,
remorse and worry fill my sleepless head.
A calmer voice, so still, so small my ear
can't hear, enfolds my lonely, lumpy bed
with comfort, whispers to my thumping heart,
"You, *you're* my child. All nature, but my art."

Sunrise on the Mountain

Swaying pine silhouettes,
needles pricking the eastern sky,
hint of approaching day.
Crimson light
soaks across the horizon.
Yellow warbler stirs in his nest
and calls softly to his mate.
Sun advances over the ridge,
burning away clouds.
Darkness retreats
beneath trees and bushes.
Dragonflies hover
on motionless air.
Gray squirrel scurries
down a stretching fir tre.
I find balm,
where sunrise
is the biggest happening
of the day.

Scene Above

Mountains silhouetted against
the sky announce dawn.
Trees, tinged with gold on one side,
cast long shadows on the grass.

The overhead screen washes
from blue to pale along the horizon line.
Birds fly past, perch on branches,
add musical accompaniment.
Up and over the mountains,
a jet paints a silent vapor trail.

The lake yawns itself awake,
puffs white splotches in the west.
The fiery sun climbs high above
and shade plays hide-and-seek,
sneaks to the opposite side of trees and buildings.
Clouds congregate
in shades of shiny white to dusky gray.
Impotent, they creep like caterpillars
toward the mountains.

The sky blazes purple and pink
reflects on the lake's stillness.
Fuzzy streaks of mauve and yellow
brush across the face of a muted sun.
The drone of a small plane's engine
and hum of mosquitoes
serenade evening's arrival.

Colors disappear. A few stars
peek through the cloud blanket.
A new episode airs tomorrow.
There are no previews or re-runs.

There's Something
about Mountains

I've crossed the great river
that divides our continent,
waded where sea and sand meet,
sailed on the sparkling ocean,
rode across the endless prairie.
Each sight brought its own delight.

Yet there's something about mountains.
Back at home, great peaks tower above me.
High meadows full of bright wildflowers,
birds soaring over pine forests,
icy streams fed by melting snow,
catch my heart and hold it.

Over the centuries, adventurers
felt the challenge and responded.
Obsessed with reaching the top, they
lived and died climbing Mt. McKinley,
the Matterhorn and Everest.

Abraham climbed the mountain
with his son Isaac and received a reprieve.
Moses talked with God on the mountain.
Mohammad and Buddha
communed on the mountain.
When seeking solitude and peace
Jesus went to the mountain.

Mountain Lure

The mountains call to me and I must go:
to hear the splash of waterfalls and rush
of wind in pines, to watch the flight of crow
and search for timid deer, who hide in brush.

    Mountains call me
    from the city
    from the desert
    from the beach.

I shall return to where the forest reigns
and air is pure and fresh: where I relax,
renew my zest for life. At any time,
the mountains call to me and I must go.

Evening at the Cabin

Mountain breezes stop worrying the trees.
Sun floods Strawberry Point with parting rays.
Blazing crimson pinnacles pose
like a royal court above the forest green.
From the deck I savor the view across the valley.
Hummingbirds contend for a place at the feeder.

My parents built this summer cabin
in retirement years. The mountainside slopes
down from the cabin to a circular driveway,
a woodpile where chipmunks chase each other,
the spot we empty fruit and vegetable scraps
to tempt wandering deer.

I breathe pine scented air, remember
roasting hot dogs and marshmallows
around the fire ring below the driveway.
Father cooked sourdough hotcakes,
bigger than plates, on his homemade griddle,
stirred sizzling chicken legs in the Dutch oven.

We ate around a small table in a grove of trees,
except one summer when wasps built a nest.
Children chased horned toads in the manzanita,
coaxed squirrels to eat peanuts from their hands,
and clambered down the slope to a swing
hidden from parents' supervision.

When lightning struck a tall pine, Father chopped
it down, sawed it into firewood, leaving only
a flat round stump. When Father was eighty-two,
he and I sat by the fire.
This is my last trip here, he declared,
as we watched the logs burn to ash.

One Fir Tree

Next to your empty chair
I decorate a fresh-cut tree,
try to create a holiday mood.

the tree top angel
we bought our first Christmas,
strings and strings of lights

(every year you bought more)
ceramic birds that once
belonged to Mother,

snowflakes tatted by a shut-in
around the corner,
a wooden gingerbread man

Karen painted,
olive wood ornaments
I purchased when we

were in Bethlehem, A bell
your sister beaded,
blown glass ornaments

you bought at an after Christmas sale,
candy cane reindeer
from a grandchild.

No new ornaments this year.

Does the forest miss this one fir tree?

Living Witnesses

Olive trees, two thousand years old,
stand in the Garden of Gethsemane,
speak to me as I stroll past:

He walked here,
knelt here.
His robe brushed our leaves.
Our branches spread over his anguish.
The words He spoke to His Father
cannot be repeated.
We saw torches coming,
heard footsteps approach,
watched the kiss of death.
We witnessed as He healed
the soldier's ear.
Our trunks bent when they led Him away.
Now we wait for His return.

The old tress, twisted and hollow,
still bear olives each autumn.

Redwood Respite

We're swallowed by a forest
of living, breathing giants.
Yesterday we endured miles
of dirt and struggling plants.
Today, moss and mushrooms cover
spongy ground where trees grow
so tall we can't see the tops –
way too big around to hug.

A mystic life force flows in this grove
removed from human stress.
There's something sacred about
sitting inside a living, hollow tree.

This place understands secrets
we could use: how to be immune
to harmful influences,
how to stand tall and stately
for 2,000 years, telling no one
what they've seen and heard,
how their intertwined root systems
support each other, how even in death
they nourish a new generation.

Driftwood

Half hidden in lilacs,
at the end of a long lane,
a piece of twisted driftwood
shoulders my mailbox --
not old-bone smooth
but rough and scarred
like a plague of eczema.

I do not know if this wood
began life on a mountainside
where cougars pounced
on their prey and bears
raised their cubs,
or if it grew in someone's
backyard where children
climbed – if it held a swing
or a snack of apples –
or if it grew in a pasture
providing shelter for cattle.

I do not know if an ax,
disease or insects felled it.

I do not know what streams
it followed, how many shores
it passed; if it floated to the ocean
or a lake, or snagged
along a river bank.

I only know that my journey
like the driftwood, will end here.

Beyond My Means

If I could count the stars that hang on peak
of night, relieve the mountains' weight of sky,
if I could read the blowing leaves and speak
the language rambling wind exhales, if I
could sing the song of cats at rest or hear
a seed begin to sprout, if I could catch
a piece of morning, paste it over a tear,
if I could ease the pain of parting, patch
the rift between two friends, if I could see
a spirit's essence, touch its filmy hand,
if I could learn the truth of sages, be
informed beyond my means, then I could stand
on higher ground and judge your careless acts,
but I, like you, am subject to the facts.

Reactivated

They call it a prayer plant,
the sisters who bring it.
Small green leaves brushed with
splotches of brown and dark green
charm the woman.

She sets it in the window,
waters it and watches it grow.
When summer explodes
she carries it outside to the flower garden
and ignores it.

Influences of the world
take their toll
in sunburned leaves, baked soil
where sprinklers miss it.

By fall,
only two scorched leaves remain.
The woman shakes her head,
almost throws it in the trash.
Instead, she sets it back in the window
feeds and waters it.

Because the plant's roots are strong,
new leaves grow fast and large.
At night they pair together
and point heaven-ward
like two hands giving thanks.

Petunia King Dies

Headline: Deseret News: June 1996

What did the petunia king look like?
Did he wear robes of deep purple
with double ruffles,
or was he just a plain
petunia of the patch?

Did he die from lack of water?
Was he eaten by snails,
or attacked by a child?
Did he breathe poison spray,
or catch some deadly disease,
or was there an assassin
hiding in the bed?
Too bad he didn't just go to seed.
That way, at least, he'd have an heir.
Now perhaps the petunias
will turn to democracy.

I must be especially considerate
of my petunias today,
knowing they have just lost their king.

Picking Raspberries

Mama sends me out to pick the raspberries.
I don a long sleeved shirt, long pants,
tie a small bucket around my waist,
leaving both hands free for picking,
put on my garden shoes and straw hat.

(The hat so I won't get freckles
like my best friend Amy.
Hers are as close as the seeds
on a raspberry.)

Ripe berries drop easily into my hands
leaving only small white knobs on the stem.
My hands and mouth are soon stained deep red.
The biggest berries hide close to the ground,
where I have to bend to reach them.
My hat gets caught in the bushes.
I toss it on the lawn.
I guess one or two freckles won't be so bad.

Thorns scratch my hands, my ankles,
my arms, when they stretch beyond the sleeves.
I come upon grasshopper skeletons
all kinds of bugs, even a big spider in a web.
I skip the berries around that one.
I empty my bucket a few times
into Mama's bowl, all the while thinking
about raspberry shortcake for dinner
and that deliciously sweet jam
on hot bread in the winter.

I don't see
the thin black ribbon winding its way
along the ground until I get to the last bush.
That's when I scream and run.
Berries dot the dirt like freckles.

Sans the Breath of Life

We have much in common,
your family and mine,
though you may not
want to claim us.

We come in black, brown,
red, yellow, white
and shades in between.
We're large and small,
old and young,
round and flat,
curvy and jagged,
slick and smooth,
or rough and unpolished.

We dwell on mountain peaks,
deserts and ocean floors.
Some of us survived
the refiner's fire,
others are content to sit,
still others are on the go.
Some stand firm
in face of adversity,
while others are tossed
about by every wind.

You collect and treasure
some of us, while trampling
the rest beneath your feet.

And, yes! We, too, were made
from dust of the earth.

Dust to Dust

"Boot Hill," my brothers name it-
this place we leave our sister.
We follow the hearse along a dusty trail
to a small hill rising from the desert floor,
just shy of the Colorado border.
No trees nor grass defy the barrenness,
as we look for miles in all directions.
Headstones and dirt mounds
mark resting places.
A few weeds atop the mounds
struggle for survival in earth
scorched by August sun.
Flowers from the funeral
seem gaudy and out of place here.
Pallbearers place the coffin over the hole.
A backhoe stands nearby
ready to cover the latest arrival.
A dirt mound marks the next spot
where Howard lies, quiet now for two years.
Children, grandchildren, siblings
share tears, hugs and words
while the casket is lowered,
then file silently back to our cars.
I empty rocks from my sandals.
Then we drive back down the dirt track
as a dry wind whirls dust heavenward.

Companions

Naming

The earth is new and clean and bright
when Adam calls all beasts in sight.
I'll give you names this very night.

They stand in line for seven hours
waiting for Eve to name the flowers.

He starts with *aardvark, ant* and *bat*
then *bear* and *buzzard, camel, cat.*
(Now Adam fears this habitat.)

Next comes the *crane* and *dog* and *duck*
Then Adam's mortal tongue gets stuck,

so Eve soon brings cold drinks for all
and he resumes his Godly call
with shaky voice, about to fall,

gazelle. He says each separate name,
iguana, rabbit, none the same,

until the dawn arrives, when fast
here comes *zebra* trotting past.
Poor Adam drops to sleep at last.

Ode to an Earthworm

You squirm
  through soil
    next to daffodil
      bulbs, never see
        their regal crowns.
      Strawberry roots
    welcome your massage
as you wiggle through,
  but you never taste
    juicy red berries.
      You loosen the dirt
        under roses,
          yet never smell
            the scent of summer.
        Petunias grow
      in your tracks
    but you never stroke
their fragile petals.
You tunnel the earth
  beneath willow trees,
    never hear
      rustling leaves.

You're acquainted
with every root, bulb,
tuber and rock,
know when to burrow
up or down,
left or right.
Your setae
grip the earth
as you
s   t   r   e   t   c   h
to inch through
packed soil,
or they anchor
you for a nap.
If some sharp-eared
robin eats half of you,
you simply grow
a new half.
You feel
the intimate
touch of naked strength
on sensitive skin.
You know

the taste and smell,
     the change
       of temperature
       and mood in
      darkness, as you slide
         through dirt
       and it slides
      through you.
       In the end,
      your five
     hearts
    mesh
   with
  that of
earth.

Party Crashers

The air-borne Draculas
        bring their
                aunts, uncles, cousins,
      grandnephews
and all the neighbors
           to the annual
   family reunion.

Even before
              invited guests
     sit down to eat,
       the party crashers
gorge themselves
     on sweet red liquid –
        Grandpa Sam's, hot,
Cousin Jill's, cold.

           Faster than Superman
      they dive, stab, suck
           and take off.
      Many sacrifice
       their lives
in a blood-thirsty
       scheme to survive.

"Got 'im!" Uncle Billy brags.
           He lifts a limp body from
    Aunt Polly's arm
          where his fingers
      raised a rosy print.
"There's one on your cheek,"
          Aunt Polly cries.
    She leans back
       and lets him have it.
They never did find the body.

Breakfast Included

I walk along the path from my motel room
to the lobby for breakfast.
The sun so bright, the sky so blue
it looks painted on.
Beside the path, a colony of ants swarm
a dead beetle. A hummingbird flits from
blossom to blossom,
hovers like a helicopter.
A squirrel scurries up a nearby Ponderosa,
its cheeks so full it can't scold.
A plastic bag full of garbage
sits outside one door.
Crows have pecked it open
and now squabble over its contents.

In the lobby I fill my plate
with eggs and ham
while I wait for my waffle to bake.
A young man at a nearby table
cleans his plate, loads a second one
with bagels, cream cheese and ham.
He puts together two sandwiches
takes a plastic bag from his pocket,
stuffs them in and walks out.
I marvel at his audacity.
When I finish my breakfast,
I take an apple and leave.

Blue Jay

Squawk! Squawk!

You can complain all you want
about my raspy call.
Not my fault – I was hatched that way.
My parents and all

my brothers screech the same.
You must admit however,
that we're the handsomest
most colorful fellas in feather.

Let me turn and spread my wings.
Notice how my bright blue
is accented with light and dark.
Watch, I'll just swoop around for you.

Hey! You drab little birds,
get outta that tree.
I'm eating them nuts.
They grow just for me!

Squawk! Squawk!

Black Feathers

1
A lonely man
rests by a brook
in a famine-ravished land.
A bird, feathers black as a pit,
brings life-sustaining food.
Though the menu may be boring,
the trips tedious for the raven,
he serves dinner daily
until the earth
again bears fruit.

2
A lonely man
sits brooding in his study
hungry for soul food
when a bird, descendant of the first,
taps on his door,
enters at his window,
departs nevermore.
Not following in the footsteps
of his fathers
this rebellious raven
brings only a mood
as black as himself.

3

One quiet afternoon,
I sit in my yard
planning a dinner menu.
A raven sits on the fence,
pierces my solitude
with his rasping caw.
Is he calling a friendly greeting,
or an omen portending doom?
I cannot tell by the fit of his feathers.

The Eagle Tree

In March the eagles swoop across our sky—
their perching place this solitary tree –
for just a week or so and then they fly.

Their heads are white; we soon identify
the species, call our friends in glee.
In March the eagles swoop across our sky.

They build no nests, though branches stretch up high,
but settle silhouetted for all to see.
for just a week or so and then they fly.

They rest awhile to feed and fortify
against the northern cold reality.
In March the eagles swoop across our sky.

In mornings when they hunt, we hear their cry
from nearby lake – a screeching cacophony--
for just a week or so and then they fly.

The watchers flock to photograph and sigh
at large majestic birds that soar so free.
In March the eagles swoop across our sky;
for just a week or so and then they fly.

Survivors

The sky is a blotted palette
of grays. Two magpies perch
on the skeleton of a poplar.
Dry leaves crackle,
as cats prowl the brown lawn.

Yellow warblers and black and white
chickadees peck berries near the porch.
Clouds darken and lower.
I turn on lights over the table,
for my snack of juice and a bun.

One magpie dives at
the cats, scolds as they crouch,
spit and cower.
Light rain begins to drizzle
dripping into afternoon.

Temperatures plummet,
rain turns to snow, and cats scratch
at the door.
White flakes blow inside while
I let the fussing felines in.

The birds have vanished,
I stand at the window, but catch
no flash of beak or feather
in the thickening chill.
Has the storm driven

them beyond night?
Next morning an unending swatch
of frozen white covers
the world. Against the pale
sky, birds cling to the power line.

Pelican View

Weak as wilted lettuce, Jenny relaxes
in her favorite chair next to the lake.
It will take weeks before she feels this good again.
Chemo steals everything except her last breath.

Water and sky mist together in a mixture of blue-grays.
A flock of pelicans splash white dots amid the ripples.
Wings held back, they tip their great beaks
beneath the water then tilt them skyward.

She might refuse to go, paint her last days peaceful
without the hours of vomiting, churning in bed.
Maybe her hair would grow back, look nice in the coffin.

The pelicans rise. With flaps and glides of powerful wings,
they fly in a line towards a distant island,
heads hunched back on shoulders,
bulging pouches resting against white feathered breasts.
One bird remains behind, still fishing. Then it rises,
flaps after the other birds with a meal for its hungry chicks.

Nine year old Megan dreams of dancing in the Nutcracker.
Andy, at six, lives for soccer and ice cream.
Ashley, barely three, breathes dolls and nursery rhymes –
all too young for the grown-up worries heaped on their plates.

A sudden gust blusters in from the lake.
Waves crash against the shore in front of Jenny.
The lone pelican beats its wings against the wind.

Heron Watch

As pink and yellow weave across the morning,
a one-eyed heron, in its usual place on the dock,
watches and waits. It cocks its head to one side,
dives after a fish – misses.

On the horizon, fishing boats ride high in the water
trailing nets. One smaller, older boat floats nearer.

A lone fisherman, ignoring the bird,
strolls to the end of the pier and throws in his line.
The heron watches and waits.

As the sun rises higher and boats become loaded
they snuggle lower into the water.
The small boat still floats high.

The fisherman reels in his line dangling a fish
and the bird makes a pass – misses.
"Ah, Snatch," the fisherman grumbles.
"You're no threat anymore."
The heron watches and waits.

Larger boats pull in to dock with full nets.
Men wield sticks to protect their catch,
as a flock of gulls try to grab fish.
After a few swoops, the heron gives up.

With his basket of fish in one hand
and his pole in the other, the fisherman heads home.
The heron watches and waits.

Just before sundown, the small boat pulls up
with a few fish and the heron lands on its weathered deck.
The old captain throws a fish to the bird.
"Here ya go, Matey," he calls,
in a voice that cracks with salt water.
Before pulling himself onto land, he adjusts his eye-patch.

Looking for Sea Turtles

on the Florida coast

I follow friends to the beach.
They claim it's the season when giant turtles
come out of the water to lay eggs.

No lights allowed, we feel our way down
wooden steps to the squishy sand,
spread out, voices low, eyes searching.

Soon I am alone, only the slow shushing
rhythm of the Atlantic, washing, washing the shore,
relinquishing abandoned shells.

An affectionate breeze strokes my chin
carries tantalizing scents of tropical isles.
Low in the east, a faint light squeezes

through the sky – at first just a glow,
then a pale ivory orb streaked
with vapor – vanishes.

We are part of each other; the sea,
the sky, the turtles, the lifeless shells
and I.

All pieces of one grand mélange.
I do not find sea turtles.
This night I find myself.

Chosen Fish

Why me?
Why did I have to be there
when God wanted
to be rid of Jonah?
Why couldn't He let the man
lie on the ocean floor
where he wouldn't bother anyone?

But no!
God said, "Swallow Jonah!"
No one else could make me do it.
I had to hold my nose
to get him down.

The guy
is too tough to digest.
It's been three days
and I still feel him
squirming in my belly.

God said,
"Swallow Jonah!"
He didn't say I had to keep him.

Below the Surface

Dolphins frolic, chase each other,
leap in great arches by the ship's waves,
entertain the passengers.
Then diving in shimmery ripples,
they disappear into a hidden world
teeming with mystery.

A wrasse picks food
from the barracuda's teeth without harm.
Electric eels generate power underwater.
A damselfish swims fearlessly
among the anemone's poison tentacles.
Only the patient oyster
polishes irritations into pearls.

Inside These Walls

We watch fish in the aquarium
at the care center
while we wait for Grandma
to finish her shower.

A tall flat angel fish moves its body
in waves as it floats past.
Small neons, their bright stripes barely visible
against the blue rocks at the bottom,
flash back and forth.

Golden fish weave in and out
of a feathery fern.
Two black mollies chase each other
round and round, up and down
then hide in a coral rock.
A silvery fish with black spots
and long feelers
swims to the surface and
then to the bottom
as if searching for food.
An orange fish with a pointy tail
nibbles on a striped plant.
A black creature with several fins
and whiskers seems attached
to the inside of the glass.

A thermometer hangs near the surface
and bubbles rise from
a treasure chest on the bottom.
A waterfall seems
to flow upward.

These glass walls allow us
a glimpse inside
the carefully controlled environment,
while keeping the fish contained
in their world.

The attendant tells us
we can visit Grandma now.

Desert Race

The lizard and road runner ran a race
across the burning sand so wide and free,
A blurry streak, a whoosh! and scarce a trace

that runners passed this barren desert place,
no sagebrush, cactus, grass nor shady tree
where lizard and road runner ran their race.

In pain the road runner wiped its face
with sagging wings, but I could only see
a blurry streak, a whoosh! and scarce a trace

in sand, that rippled like fancy crocheted lace.
The sun burned hot enough to melt the sea
when lizard and road runner ran their race.

The lizard scurried, quickened his frantic pace.
Then faster, faster, faster they ran, and Whee!
a blurry streak, a whoosh! and scarce a trace

that shifting whining winds would soon erase,
just leaving sand, bare sand. Can it be
that lizard and road runner ran a race -
a blurry streak, a whoosh! and left no trace?

No Answer

A little girl with bows in her hair
took the last of Charcoal's kittens today.
She rubbed her face on the tiny gray fur ball,
promised to take good care of her.
I felt lucky to find homes
for five kittens; couldn't keep them,
didn't want to take them to the pound.

Alan was *my* first to leave,
on a mission to Pennsylvania.

The black male went to a widow,
looking for company.

Bonnie married, still lives in town
but gone from here.

A farmer, needing a mouser,
took one of the spotted females.

Vince moved out,
bought a trailer.

The smallest spotted kitten found a home
with a newly-married couple.

Lon flew all the way to Tahiti
when he left.

A man from the nursing home
took the gray male.

Yesterday I watched Mark
board the plane for Winnipeg.

Charcoal prowls this empty house,
mewing. There is no answer.
Tonight she and I curl together
in front of the fireplace.

Forest Encounter

One September morning
I walk the road from the cabin,
turn a corner, come upon a young buck.
Startled, we both stop
in the middle of the road
about ten feet apart.
We stare at each other.
He, long ears and tail alert
black nose testing the air.
I scarcely breathe,
afraid he'll spring away.

I speak softly,
"Hello there.
You're a handsome fellow."
He doesn't return my compliment,
stands like a bronze statue,
proud head erect.
I move my hand ever so slowly,
bring my camera into position.
He is gone.
My scrapbook moment vanished
among aspen and pine.

A few more weeks
and the hunters will come.

Song of the Camels

It's step by step and night on night we go
across the barren sand from water hole to well.
The long awaited star's our guide. We know

we carry heavy gifts. Our pace is slow.
It's gold, and frankincense and myrrh that smell.
It's step by step and night on night we go

through heat and danger, swaying by in a row
to Bethlehem, past dune and sandy swell.
The long awaited star's our guide. We know

the journey's long, and desert winds will blow
to shift the sand; a place where robbers dwell.
It's step by step and night on night we go

to find the Holy Child and then bestow
the gifts on Him who'll save us all from Hell.
The long awaited star's our guide. We know

we'll see Him soon, with Heaven's Holy Glow.
They'll celebrate with song and flute and bell.
It's step by step and night on night we go.
The long awaited star's our guide. We know!

Liquid Assets

Controller of the World

Lack or overabundance
of this natural resource
destroys civilizations,
more surely than invading armies.
It surrounds us, above,
on and beneath the earth,
even inside our bodies.

From tiny droplets
to Neptune's vast domain,
from vapor to icebergs,
water wears many faces.

As a toddler I splashed in the bathtub,
went out of my way to stomp in puddles,
ran through the sprinkler on the lawn.
Later I made snowmen,
swam, ice skated and cruised.

Though man has tried rain dances,
water witching. harnessed its energy,
dammed and diverted it into canals,
only its Maker can truly control water.
Ask Noah, Moses or Elijah.

Rainy Season

Drops fall like silver knives,
slice my memories into vignettes.

dancing barefoot in the rain
until our clothes and hair dripped
heavy as mud

splashing through all the puddles
on the way home from school
seeing who could find the most worms

running for the last bus in a spring storm
my hand in yours
a wet kiss at the door

you holding the umbrella
as we dashed to the hospital
the night Johnny was born

burying Mom in soggy ground
drying my eyes
on your handkerchief

This rain, more menacing,
slashes my face, stabs my heart.

You are not here.

Summer Storm

This early morn, a cloud form sneaks
along the highest mountain peaks.

More shapes appear to swallow sun.
The thirsty-throated thunder speaks
in growly notes. The cougars run

when jagged knives of lightning slice
the sky, and wind lashes spruce
and aspen. The squirrels, deer and mice
all hide while water pelts the moose

and flattens grass. Then grayness steals
away, unmasking bits of blue.
The shadow rumbles east, reveals

a forest strengthened after strain
of lightning, wind and saving rain.

Afternoon Storm

Great gray clouds rise from the west,
boil, churn, swallow the sun.
The air rumbles and cracks.
Hail slices leaves from tomato vines,
shreds bright petunia blossoms.
Branches of the old maple tree
lash against a corner of the house.
With a great gust a large limb wrenches free
and dances in frenzy across the street.

Inside, an old man sips a warm bowl of soup,
stirs the smoldering fire,
settles into his recliner for a nap.
Roused by a thump against the front window,
he stands, hobbles to open the door.
Wind and hail greet him.
The man's eyes search the ground
beneath the window.
A lump of crumpled feathers
lies almost buried by hail.
He limps towards it,
the storm forcing him against the house.
Gently he gathers the warm, still body
in one big, misshapen hand.
Fighting the wind, he carries it inside,
places it on a warm towel on the hearth.
strokes wet feathers,
remembers storms.

Storm Sonata

Alone, with twenty miles of swirling snow,
dense fog and icy roads ahead of me,
I grip the steering wheel and strain to see
through evening darkness turning white. Although
I've traveled here before, tonight I know
confusion. Wipers click disharmony –
don't help. I search to find the willow tree
that tells me where to turn. I inch on slow

and push the radio. "You'll Never Walk
Alone" begins to comfort and calm my fear.
Then "Edelweiss" soon follows. Here's my street.
It's been an hour; it's almost ten o'clock.
With strains of "Goin' Home," my driveway near,
grand music calms and makes return complete.

Ripples on the Pond

Charlie shuffles down a worn path
lets himself down slow
on a big rock at the edge of the pond.
His breath comes in short puffs
as bright air wraps him in pine freshness.

His right hand
reaches down, curls around
a smooth flat pebble.
*Still the best skipping stones
in the country.*
He rolls the rock between shaky fingers.

When he was ten
he could skip a stone clear to the other side
farther than Eddie or Sam.
Sometimes he fished here with his dad
slow and quiet.
He swam here with Alice
carved their initials in a heart
on a young aspen.

Charlie lifts his eyes
searches for the aspen;
nothing left but a rotted stump.
He lets the stone drop to the ground
pushes and pulls himself to his feet
and hobbles back up the path.

A cold wind makes ripples on the pond.

Downstream

When Margaret discovered the light,
she turned her life over to God.
She carefully weeded out unworthy thoughts,
raked her mind free of garbage,
purged dark hidden memories
of black deeds.

Gathering all the evil into a wagon
she pulled it to the river.
With one great heave she tipped the load,
spilled the trash into swirling eddies.
She watched until the last trace
disappeared beneath the surface
and the current carried it away.
She flew homeward, rejoicing.

Downstream, Margaret's children splashed,
waded, where water flowed slow and shallow.

No Footprints

Our seaplane follows the shoreline
along Kenai Peninsula. Low tide now,
the ocean leaves a muddy flat
below rails and highway.

Accompanied by roar of engines,
we fly between mountain peaks,
a wilderness of white and green.
Mountain sheep cling to rocky ledges

between ice fields, glaciers, waterfalls.
Near the glacier in Prince William Sound,
our pilot finds a space between kayaks
and floating ice, sets the plane on the water,

shuts off engines. Even a whisper seems
an intrusion in the vast stillness. I expect
the glacier to be smooth, shiny gray-white.
Instead it's wrinkled, cracked, striated blues,

pinks, greens –a frozen bulldozer –
carving its relentless passage to the sea.
I step out on the runner, take a few photos.
A chunk of ice breaks off, plunges into

the Sound. The pilot hurries me back
into the plane, explains, "Vibrations from
the propellers sometimes cause ice to crack
and break off." He starts the engines,

treads water a short distance, and we're
airborne. Ripples vanish, along with
our shadow. Evidence we've been here
imprinted only in our knowing.

Troubled Waters

The sea rolls restless this evening –
no huge waves crashing at my feet,
yet the water seems troubled,
as if Neptune may be stretching,
planning his next attack.
Water nymphs dance
across the ripples.

I walk beside this water
that has stolen so much from me.
Some hypnotic force
propels me here.

The beach house
which nurtured my childhood
became this sea's victim –
swallowed whole.
Another stormy day,
my father with his heavy coat,
great long boots, and shaggy beard
disappeared in his fishing boat,
leaving only memories.

Tonight the sun slowly slips into the sea
robbing me of my last light.

Neptune's Surplus

The water washed upon the sandy shore,
spewed debris – an outgrown shell, a weed –
all tossed from Neptune's underwater store,

heaved across the beach where dogs explore,
where hermit crabs and squawking gulls can feed.
The water washed upon the sandy shore

and left an oil slick, a broken oar,
a piece of coral, a cork, a twisted reed –
all tossed from Neptune's underwater store.

He secrets wealth beneath shadows murky door –
a ship, the pirate's gold, a pearly bead.
The water washed upon the sandy shore

a plank, a dying fish, an apple core,
a rusty bolt, a shoe, a pomegranate seed –
all tossed from Neptune's underwater store.

His demons sort and stack, make room for more
and cast aside the things he will not need.
The water washed upon the sandy shore
stuff tossed from Neptune's underwater store.

Hurricane!

The whirling tempest blew ashore last night.
It toppled trees and snapped the power poles
like straws in milk. The moon withheld its light.
In dark, we fled to higher rocky knolls,

> listened
> to our homes groan
> as rushing waves
> split them open.

We heard the crushing water swallow past
and future, gulp on thirsty gulp, as wind
kept urging, pushing, driving ever on.
The whirling tempest blew ashore last night.

Drawn from the Nile

A baby hid among the reeds
soon whimpers loud for mother-care.
The princess hears and finds and feeds
the baby hid among the reeds.
She names the boy, supplies his needs,
rescues from the Pharaoh's snare
that baby hid among the reeds
who whimpered loud for mother-care.

When Hebrew people groan in pain
Jehovah hears their anguished plea.
A fiery bush across the plain—
when Hebrew people groan in pain.
Moses, chosen to break the chain
of bondage, sets the Hebrews free.
When Hebrew people groan in pain
Jehovah hears their anguished plea.

Hail and frogs and lice and flies—
Pharaoh, let the people go!
The king resists, so Moses tries
hail and frogs and lice and flies.
A last resort—the first son dies.
Ram's long horns begin to blow.
Hail and frogs and lice and flies—
then Pharaoh lets the people go!

Pursued by soldiers, Hebrews walk
on barren land between the waves.
The waters rush on top and shock
pursuing soldiers. Hebrews walk
until the water flows from rock.
When people falter, Moses saves.
Pursued by soldiers, Hebrews walk
on barren land between the waves.

A fearful people journey home,
fed from above without a flaw.
A pillar of fire and clouds like foam
lead the fearful people home.
For forty years the Hebrews roam.
They must learn to live The Law.
A fearful people journey home,
fed from above without a flaw.

Hallowed Waters

Waters trickle down the slopes
of Mt. Hermon, dash downhill, merge
and become a meandering river

feeding fertile fields, vineyards,
citrus and olive trees
and an abundance of fish

as they flow into the Sea of Galilee.
Leaving the low end of this lake,
Jordan River continues southward.

Children of Israel followed
the Ark of the Covenant through the river
on dry ground, water piled on both sides.

Two prophets walked between its waves,
and Elijah rode a flaming chariot to heaven,
while Elisha watched from the bank.

Naaman, the Syrian, bathed
seven times in the river,
was cured of leprosy.

In a secluded spot, John the Baptist
washed away sins of believers
and baptized the Savior of the world.

Jordan River empties into the Dead Sea.
With no place to go, even living waters die,
wafted to Heaven by desert winds.

On the Shores of Galilee

A hush before the dawn awakes this day.
The shackled breezes wait for lift of night's
dark curtain. Water laps the shore, the way
a mother strokes her baby. Golan Heights
appear across the sea, as sky turns pale.
Like James and Peter, fishermen will take
their nets, untie the boats, prepare to sail
once more and fish this ancient, flowing lake.
The sun soon peers above a ridge and sends
one ray to streak the water. Seagulls start
their daily search for bread. A group of friends
will gather, watch the fishermen depart.
The morning's bright with promise, air is fresh
with scent of sea and land and living flesh.

At dusk the troubled waters churn and boil.
High crashing waves reflect small sparks of light.
The storm has grasped a boat. Its sailors toil
to bring her in. There's none aboard with might,
authority, to order wind to stop
its blowing, calm the waves and save the crew;
and none with faith enough to step atop
the rolling waters, walk to shore. Then through
the mist appears a beam of light, a path
amid the storm as smooth as sand. The cheer
from shore is stilled by tempest's windy wrath.
The vessel docks; the men are safe. Bare fear
and wonder shine from eyes, and we all know
that Living Water robbed the undertow.

Antelope Island

Pioneers on the island understood:
Great Salt Lake is moody as
an old man with rheumatism.
Salty, mountain man Jim Bridger
declared it part of the Pacific Ocean.

Yesterday a smooth mirror: playground
for swimmers, boaters,
enough tiny black flies to swarm
the shores and cover
the beach, a good day for brine-

shrimpers. Squawking gulls begged,
followed me for hand-outs.
After a rocky climb
to the lookout, on the far
shore I spotted a lone heron.

Today the lake is a rumpled
quilt of grays. Green banded ducks
ride the billows. Watery fingers comb
the beach smooth. The misty air
breathes salt in

my nostrils, rattles a loose board
on the abandoned ranch house.
Ahead of the approaching storm,
a deer leads her fawns to higher
ground. Rabbits remain hidden.

Tomorrow maddened
waves will chew at the causeway, spray plumes
over anyone who ventures to come.
Buffalo will huddle, woolly sides together.
Dashing waters may waken

bones sleeping on the lake bed:
unwary sailors, pilots,
the old rancher rowing home
with medicine for his wife, other
ghosts, and perhaps claim a fresh one.

No Return

Life is a waterfall and we
are drops of water, pushed
over the edge by our mothers'
bodies. Most of us form bonds,
holding hands with first

one drop and then another.
Those few who shun fellowship
spray off on their own,
lost as mist in forgotten places.
We cannot resist the pull

of gravity, ever downward.
Rocks along the way cause
constant change in our course,
and companions. Immovable
obstacles we maneuver around;

others we shove out of our way.
While a few drops reach
the pool in only a minute,
some may take
a hundred years.

Our destination is inevitable.
In the end we plunge
into that joyous, welcoming dance
with those who went before
and those who follow after.

Sea Waltz

The sea is calling me from depths below.
I feel its tug inside my soul. My face
is turned to smell its breath, although
it cannot penetrate this desert place.

The sea is pulling me with mystic force
beyond my own. I feel the pulse of waves
inside my veins and know that nature's course
still leads all creatures downward to their graves.

The sea is bidding me to come and rest,
to lay my cares upon its shore, and let
my shell be washed away atop its crest,
to dance among its creatures free and wet.

Oh, take me to the sea when I must die.
There let my spirit waltz with sea and sky.

Rotation

Nothing Stands Still

Man feels this constant drive
to be on the move –
motorcycles, jeeps, buses, trains –
engines burning, burning.

Always he is in motion,
coming, going, leaving, returning –
canoes, yachts, ferry boats, cruise ships–
water churning, churning.

Whether he's in New York, Cairo or Hong Kong,
he wants to be somewhere else –
Cessnas, helicopters, jets, rockets,
endless yearning, yearning.

It's no fault of man really.
Blame it on his Creator
who placed him on this planet
in a solar system, turning, turning.

January Confinement

This two-faced month drags
you from past over
threshold of future.
Once in his icy
clasp you are sentenced
to thirty-one long
nights of his bleak
companionship, dark days
of blizzards spiced with
autumn's death rattle.

Though you plead your case,
January grants
no pardons. When you
feel him stalking, arm
yourself with blankets,
robes, furry slippers,
scented candles, soft
music, bubble bath,
flowers, chocolate
and some good poems.

Cold Clutches

It creeps in every open crack and space
with frosty fingers, clinging icy toes.
Bold January grips this northern place

and carries snow which drifts around and blows
then covers gardens, lawns and flower beds
with frosty fingers, clinging icy toes.

The people wear their coats and cover heads
with knitted caps against the biting cold
which covers gardens, lawns and flower beds.

Thick ice now clogs the fishing holes. I'm told
I should provide my pedigreed toy dogs
with knitted caps against the biting cold.

Inside I build a fire, add more logs,
for coldness must not reach my hearth or heart.
I shall surround my pedigreed toy dogs,

my family and friends with warmth of art
to creep in every open crack and space
for coldness must not reach my hearth or heart
while January grips this northern place,

Winter-blue Days

My father taught me the beauty
of winter-blue days –
how sky hung lower, deeper,
more intense than in summer –
how sky danced on top of crusted snow
and played peek-a-boo in frosted trees
until the world turned blue –
how river echoed sky
and trees in still water –
how frozen grasses and snow
crunched beneath our feet –
how biting air pinked
our cheeks and noses
as we walked, parka'd
and mitten'd against the cold.
We gathered pieces of pitch
for the fireplace.
Inside, we sipped hot chocolate
and popped corn while
we warmed tingling toes
by the fire.

Time flowed with the river
and my teacher is gone.
Now,
as I watch burning logs
and nibble popcorn,
I share this winter-blue day
with my father.

Melt Down

The snow melted last week,
uncovering winter-brown lawn.
Black icy lumps lining roadsides
ran into storm drains.
Bird tracks, paw marks,
even the biggest footprints
disappeared.

Only temporary –
this purging of earth stains.

Today a new layer
bathes our world
in a cover so pure, so white
it lights the night.

Contamination begins again.
The fresh layer becomes stained,
turns yellow, brown and black.
Pollution layers on
one dirty sin upon another.

until Easter sets us free.

March Morning

Daylight stretches longer now
though mountains huddle
under their white winter comforters.

Lilac twigs sport pale green swellings,
and green splotches repeat on the lawn
surrounding a patch of violets.

Daffodil and tulip leaves
pry through moist soil,
joining early crocuses.

One puffy robin perches on a bare branch
next to the remains of an ill-fated kite.
A cold blast hurls snow against my window.

The aroma of fresh baked bread teases
and I take it from the oven.

It's Spring

Rooster wakes the sun a bit earlier.
Bees breakfast on prepared blossoms,
and meadowlarks resume choir rehearsal.
In anticipation of parenthood,

swallows build nests, practice diving.
Willows model new gowns,
waltz with the cottonwoods,
to shake winter doldrums.

Violets stipple the lawn.
Ducks lead their young to the pond,
while lambs crowd the sheep pen
and sprouts jump in the vegetable garden.

Seagulls follow the farmer's plow
assured of an easy meal.
Abandoned kites decorate trees, wires,
while lilac air breathes promises.

Vixen Spring

That elusive enchantress
lured me out of doors with
her warm fragrant breath,

dazzled me with a leafy ballet,
bewitched me with a feathered choir,
intoxicated me with ripe strawberries,
seduced me on a bed of violets,

then slapped
my face
with cold rain.

Evening in the Park

You left me in the springtime.
Lilacs scented purple breath through the park
and bruised my heart.
Meadowlarks' notes hung in the air.

Lilacs scented purple breath through the park,
here at the waterfall where we first met.
Meadowlarks' notes hung in the air,
as we held hands and whispered goodbyes.

Here at the waterfall where we first met
spray misted our faces with coolness.
We held hands and whispered goodbyes,
not knowing when, or if we might meet again.

Spray misted our faces with coolness.
I searched your eyes for some hope.
Not knowing when, or if we might meet again,
parting became most difficult.

I searched your eyes for some hope.
April hummed around us;
parting became most difficult.
Pigeons pecked for crumbs on the walk.

April hummed around us;
sunny forsythia seemed to mock our pain.
Pigeons pecked for crumbs on the walk,
as the black blanket of night fell.

Sunny forsythia seemed to mock our pain.
and bruised my heart,
as the black blanket of night fell.
You left me in the springtime.

Summer Dawn

The summer dawn is pure delight.
With beams and streaks and wisps of air,
it chases shadows into night.

The forest stretches, greets the sight,
with deer, a mouse, a fox, a bear.
The summer dawn is pure delight.

The rosy yellow clouds soon write
their names across the heavens. There
they chase the shadows into night.

A meadowlark begins her flight,
a trill of joy, without a care.
The summer dawn is pure delight.

The eastern sky reflects the light.
While cougars only crouch and stare,
it chases shadows into night.

The sun appears; and shines so bright,
prepared to take on any dare.
The summer dawn is pure delight.
It chases shadows into night.

Summer Snow

I sat entranced
as Daddy drove
into Cottonwoods Campground
for our Sunday picnic.
Tiny seeds insulated in white fluff
filled the mountain air.
We children raced to catch them.
They landed in the nearby gurgling brook,
on our hair, our plates,
and in our Kool-Aid.
Mama was not pleased.

Years later, cottonwoods
grow in my yard.
Afternoon warmth launches
puffs on the wind.
Neighbors complain
of allergies, white drifts
on their lawns and walks,
cotton in their cars and houses.

I see only
magic summer snow
in the canyon.

Individual Retirement Account

Long summer surely begs for lazy days.
I lounge and read and swizzle lemonade
while noon extends to evening. Party trays
are ready-made to serve beneath the shade
of trellised vines. When sunset fades, the moon
embroiders clouds with sequined thread and weaves
enchanted dreams. The garden crickets tune
their harps. When morning wakes, the maple leaves
will filter early dawn. A robin's song
begins at daylight. I won't mind the gold
on pumpkins, purple grapes, for I belong
to summer. I can smile when wind is cold.

I've saved the warmest picnics, blooms and dew
to brighten stormy hours 'til winter's through.

Gathering Season

When summer gulps
her last red apple,
and brittle leaves fly,
ranchers round up sheep and cattle,
herd them into winter pasture.

Farmers harvest corn, burn the fields,
dig potatoes and sugar beets,
pick pumpkins and apples.

Housewives hoard peaches
in mason jars,
unearth dahlia bulbs
to keep them from freezing.
Children rake leaves,
stuff them in fat plastic bags.

I have no herds, fields or trees,
so
I gather words,
pile them into poems and stories
where they will nourish me
and keep me warm.

Interlude

Between scenes of exciting
summer crowds and haunting
winter hunger, the forest
takes a lazy intermission.

Sunlight filters through
golden scrim of aspens,
between proscenium arch of pines.
Tourists have gone home,

children, back to school.
In the deserted cyclorama
a deceptive quiet prevails,
as nights stretch longer and cooler.

A hawk circles, searching in vain
for a squirrel not yet snugged
into its nest. Wrens have relocated
to sing in summer stock.

Only the winter cast remains:
the next act begins
when an early storm
blows onto center stage.

Early Snow

Bare limbs spread unashamed.
The cottonwoods are ready –
leaves molding on the lawn.

More modest maples and ash
cling to their covering,
unwilling to let go.

Ruthless snow piles on,
breaks branches across power lines,
leaves residents cold and dark.

Dahlia bulbs shiver in the ground
while tulip and daffodil, still in the bag,
huddle on a shelf in the garage

near unmounted snow tires.
Tomato vines and corn stalks
clutter the garden.

Patio furniture sports a coat of white,
while an ice crusted rose weeps
for a summer not quite finished.

Autumn Singing Trees

The whishing song of autumn-singing trees
can drown the sobs of daisies doomed to die
and warn of wicked winter's coming freeze.

This morning brings a northern turn of breeze,
and still we hear above the swan's last cry
the whishing song of autumn-singing trees.

The eagles, geese, the robins, wrens and bees
begin to fill October's sunny sky
and warn of wicked winter's coming freeze.

Fast-waning summer falls to scarlet knees
when hearing leaves repeat the lullaby –
the whishing song of autumn-singing trees.

We picnic, hike and fish and hunt to squeeze
the last remaining warmth from earth, then sigh
and warn of wicked winter's coming freeze.

With branches bare, the rowdy rustlings cease
and snow begins to whirl. I'd like to buy
the whishing song of autumn-singing trees
that warn of wicked winter's coming freeze.

October Rain

Accompanied by heaven's drums in grand
parade, a jagged flashing splits the sky,
unleashing walls of water, raising high
to thoroughly drench this parched and thirsty land –
a land that's gulping every welcome drop.
The colored waves of soggy leaves enhance
dim light, which sifts between the clouds' proud prance.
Fresh rain rejuvenates the lawns that sop
new strength, if only temporary. Frost
arrives too soon to claim its yearly due.
This fragile fall proclaims a dying year.
Flamboyant hues of autumn will be lost,
the leaves will drop and flowers die on cue,
as late October sheds its final tear.

The Wooded Path

I tread the wooded path alone tonight –
the one we strolled together long ago.
Tall maples stood as witness of delight.

Bright buds were bursting; air was filled with light.
The eagles soared above the river's flow.
I tread the wooded path alone tonight.

In youth, our promised future shone so bright.
You held my hand; I basked in heady glow.
Tall maples stood as witness of delight.

I sensed no threat of loss or pain or fright,
in shared embraces, kisses, soft and slow.
I tread the wooded path alone tonight.

Then, only NOW reflected in my sight.
How soon the end of bliss, I could not know
when maples stood as witness of delight.

I pull my coat against the frigid bite
of icy blowing spits of stinging snow,
where maples stood as witness of delight.
I tread the wooded path alone tonight.

Ode to Survival

I

They meet around my feeder every fall,
the finches, chickadees and warblers too,
until a thieving band of starlings frightens all
my welcome guests; but they return a few
at once when hunger gnaws. As winter comes
and ground is white with snow, they congregate,
converse and argue. Warblers sing and feed
my soul. The humble finches peck some crumbs
from top of frozen snow. A storm won't wait
and birds are swirled away with frightening speed.

II

Two days ago, a hungry deer digressed
and wandered to our yard. Her cupboard bare,
she looked for nourishment here. Browsing best
and lowest trees, she raised her head to stare
at us, her empty belly deep in snow.
The neighbors called her *Nuisance,* threw a stone.
I gathered kitchen scraps and set where ice
was hard. She licked them up, and turned to go.
Today three deer arrive. Somewhere a lone
timber wolf begins to howl – once, twice.

III

Inside, I watch the falling snow. I see
the morning paper lying on my walk
I hurry out. A frosted maple tree
shakes snow in front of me. A squawking flock
of starlings scatter. Wind comes, whips my face
with sleet. I slip and slide, grab a post.
My neighbor comes to help. We collect mail,
paper, walk at crawly turtle pace.
I thank her, smile as pale as any ghost.
Inside again, I hear the tempest wail.

Through the Crack

When winter blasts the land with icy breath
it grabs the earth in frosty-fisted grasp.
Its very presence breathes a painful death
for tender life. The flowers only gasp
and go, while moving creatures seek reprieve
by finding shelter, try to stay ahead
of swiftly stalking menace. Some relieve
their cold and hunger pains, stay well fed.
Anticipating coming time of want,
we work to fill our ample storage bin.
When hungry wolves and buzzards start to haunt
then even best laid plans don't always win.
There comes a time when life seeps through the crack
and winter claims us for his hoary sack.

Midnight December 31

I've written the last word.
Page 365 is finished.
The book is closed
and there is no going back.
I can revise nothing,
though I'd like to rewrite
parts of it – make it kinder,
more full of love and gratitude,
less pain and regrets.

As I begin a new book,
I try to remember what I've learned.
Despite advice of writers' guides
to get it all down fast,
in this case it seems to work better
to use my head before my pen –
better to edit before inking.
Still, one cannot see the end
from the beginning.

Last Season

A season of sorrows creeps across the earth.
Soft glow of autumn crumbles under foot.
Cold windy wails rattle brittle branches.
Gloomy shadows rumble overhead,
and darkness swallows hours of light. Some ravens
huddle, silent inky dots on power
lines. The swallows leave, the bears retreat
to lairs, the squirrels sleep, and even snakes
all disappear. The ice caps melt. The soil
shakes and rocks the cities, mountains fall
and oceans leap beyond their bounds. Hugh fires
destroy the forests. Disease and hunger stalk
the streets as people slip to frozen sleep.
Unlucky ones awake to hungry dawn.
The nations fight against each other. Men
now rob their neighbors, murder their mothers, abuse
their children, ravage the earth to satisfy greed.
Somewhere, amid the evil, shines the light
of truth and peace to wait Thy Coming Lord.